YEAR of the Cicada

MEI-MEI HOLLAND

Further Praise for

YEAR of tHE CiCADA

"A gorgeous and haunting woven tapestry of poetry and prose."

—Anne Liu Kellor, author of *Heart Radical*

"Year of the Cicada is a hybrid work from a hybrid soul.... In these pages, 'a new dimension becomes visible,' as the connections between strangers, lands, and insects are laid bare."

—Leanne Dunic, author of *One and a Half of You*

"In this stunning collection which ribbons between lyrical prose and distilled poems like quiet glass bells, Mei-Mei Holland tenderly elucidates the experience of trying to find oneself within the spaces of intergenerational trauma and the power of legacy.... A powerfully rendered metamorphosis we are privileged enough to honor alongside her."

—Addie Tsai, author of *Unwieldy Creatures*

ISBN: 978-1-938841-25-5

Book designer: Nicole Roberts
Cover art illustrator: Katie So

This book is also available in electronic book format.
Holland, Mei-Mei

Year of the Cicada / Holland

For my mom,

and her mom

"We must trace it from its ascent to its death,
when it is soon succeeded by a new generation."

Notes on the Locusta
Dr. Nathaniel Potter
Baltimore, Maryland
1839

4

CONTENTS

I. EMERGE

"[The eggs] are so transparent that we can see indistinctly the features of the future insect through the shell ..."

Twelve

First time Mom said
her mother killed herself

I was in the back seat of the car
in the Montgomery Mall parking lot

Same year Mom said–*I liked being twelve but
I don't much like listening to it*

I cried in startled anger–*Pearl
didn't want to meet me?*

As if a sour granddaughter
had weighed heavy on her mind

O O O

I was twelve when the cicadas came. They showed up on mailboxes and on chain-link fences, littered all across the streets and yards. Sometimes in their corporeal ink ugliness, sometimes just the shriveled browning remnant of a body they'd once worn.

The neighbor across the street baked them into cookies and diced them up in tacos without telling her three daughters. She was the kind of lady who gave out raisins and toothbrushes at Halloween.

At school I would laugh at blond boys wearing soccer jerseys who offered to put cicadas in their mouths for dares, exchanged for lurid truths.

Sometimes you would see them, the cicadas, in the very act of leaving their old bodies behind. Transformation, it turned out, was a gruesome thing to watch, and it left grotesque remains.

I don't know what happened to all those semi-carcasses. They couldn't have stayed around more than a few weeks. Did something eat them? Did they decay? I do not remember. One day they were gone.

Sister
a ghazal

Madeline as in the French orphan girl tended by a Sister,
Mei-Mei as in Chinese for Little Sister.

Madeline, who was not afraid of anything, not even the tiger
at the zoo,
Lived with eleven other little girls, none of them her sisters.

Her hair was red, and I collected dolls with scars across their
bellies where they used
To have appendices, and lorded my shelf full of them over my
two sisters.

Mary Magdalene, who Madeline and I were named for, didn't
even know
How to keep her frock immaculate. I think of her as Mary's
ugly stepsister.

But I heard Jesus loved her anyhow, sat her by his side and
Forgave her all her trespasses. Welcomed her, Prodigal Sister.

Mei-Mei was unplanned, I think, a Chinese name that stuck to
me when Auntie came to stay.

Chinese didn't stick to my Big Sister, or to my Even Smaller
   Sister.

At school they called me Madeline. Those kids didn't even
   know
That to the neighborhood I was Mei-Mei—'Meim' to my
   parents and my sisters.

o O O

My mother's great aunt, Auntie, used to smell like talcum powder and wore lavender bifocal glasses. She's a curved lady in my memory, back bent like a bonnet shell. *You're my Miss America*, she would say to my older sister Jenny, holding both her hands in both her hands.

And you, she'd say, taking both my hands, *you are my Miss China.* I was mildly annoyed to be receiving what was clearly a consolation prize, but I was used to Jenny getting first dibs on everything by then.

By the time my little sister Lizzy was old enough to be named after a beauty queen, maybe four or five or so, Auntie took both her hands in both her hands and said: *And you, little one, you are my Miss Chocolate.*

This made Auntie and her husband Dr. Young gasp and sigh with laughter. And then I felt better about getting Miss China after all, and I pitied Lizzy that there was no country left for her to reign.

Pearl, imagined

Mom always has beautiful
long fingernails. We lie
together in her bed,
my sisters, mom, and me.

It works like this, Mom says.
Your genes will load the gun,
your life will fire it. So keep
your fingers clean and off of triggers.

I take the extra pillows and
I hold them in between my knees
to be sure there is nowhere left to rest
for the woman rocking silent in the corner,

dark hair melting into gray,
palms dripping black with bullet grease.

II. HATCH

*"The embryo assumed the form of a worm, without legs,
and a thicker cream colour succeeded to the shining, pearl-like white
..."*

O Ò O

We thought we were like the Jetsons of a kind—
had left behind the naive trappings of a former
age, landed on a planet where the past was past
and love was universal. And we thought we
were beautiful.

The New York Times said it was our generation.
TIME magazine had a woman on the front, a
syncretization of every race from every corner.
My sixth-grade teacher handed it to me and
said, *Look, isn't she beautiful?* And I thought
it was our era.

In high school I saw a photo of a boy who
looked like me—same dark hair, skin a famil-
iar shade of beige, eyes that must have been
about halfway between his mom's shape and
his dad's. Underneath his photo he had written:
I'm the same as every other person in 2500.

And I thought, *Yes, how fortunate we, to be
ahead of schedule toward the inevitable divorce
of people from all places and from history.* We
could live in space, and we could breathe up
here.

Little Red at age 15

First man who ever touched my chest
looked fortyish or so, with long black curls

and teeth too long and wide.
He had a studio with walls and lights and cameras.

I stood in it with turquoise underwear around my ankles,
my dress an exoskeleton, empty on the ground.

How did I get here, my skin gleaming
like the turkey quiet on the counter

on a November afternoon?
He'd layered oil on in circles for the camera

until my back began to sway and I
was too afraid to speak.

Why had I stopped as I walked down the street?
I had thought that he might make me taller

and more beautiful.
I didn't understand that he meant

Stand here, darling paper doll,
and leave the rest to me.

After a country, nothing else

We called him Dr. Young, though I couldn't tell you what he
    was a doctor of.
Philosophy? Medicine? Whatever it was, it was in the old
    country.

He met Auntie at the graveyard where each came every Sunday,
thighs sticky with perspiration from off the wooden pews.

Auntie had gone to visit Uncle, and Dr. Young his own
    deceased wife,
the two of whom were neighbors in eternity.

They wed when Auntie had turned seventy, and Dr. Young was
    older still,
and moved together into one of two apartments that were his,

side by side on the third floor of a corner building.
I do not remember a single specific word exchanged between
    me and Dr. Young.

But I remember the apartment that they lived in smelled of
    Auntie
and had a flowered porcelain dish of sugar-crusted Peachie-O's

that I was always offered. And I remember Dr. Young at
   Thanksgiving dinner,
remember his suspenders, how he would burp without offering
   excuse,

how once in the tide shift between dinner and dessert, he took
   out a pen from his breast pocket
and began to write a poem in characters that I could neither
   read nor understand,

vertical lines bleeding on a ruffled paper napkin. Only once I
   crossed the threshold
of the second apartment, the one where Auntie did not live.

Dr. Young was seeking something for my father, an article or
   a device,
some object of adulthood that I didn't yet have use for. I stood
   for a moment in the foyer

and understood that I should leave. The yellowing overhead
   fell down
on a stack of newspapers up to my collarbones and then another

and another, and a carton full of fabrics—houndstooth, tweed,
   jersey, silk—
that had begun to curdle and to fray and hanging racks and
   bags and magazines and frames

and an unnamable stench crawled toward me from the inner
    rooms
and nowhere could I see the lip where the walls adjoined the
    floor.

I backed into the hallway, having lost sight of my father in the
    stalagmites and the spume.
I sat back down at the Thanksgiving table and I looked at Dr.
    Young,

his graying hair, his mushroom-colored moles, unruly strands
    growing
from his eyebrows and his ears. As I cleared the dessert plates,
    I spirited away his napkin

to unfold and lay out on my comforter that night, picking away
    the gravy at the corners,
trying to make sense of all the boxes and the lines. See for
    myself

how porous all the inky symbols were. Faulty, gap-toothed
    fishing net,
incapable of holding on to anything.

Profanity

You lit a candle on your bedside table
as on a wax-dripped corner altar

said your last girlfriend had wanted to go there
on the basement couch in front of the TV

but you'd imagined something different.
Weeks ago, you had parked around the corner

from my house, inched quietly through
the kitchen, dining room, and up the stairs.

Hid behind my door when my mother rose
and roamed the halls, sure that she had heard

a creaking of the floors. I sent you back
into the darkness, too spooked to then grow

quiet and grow soft on the quilting of my
childhood. By the time you lit that candle,

your parents were out to dinner for the evening
and we were dancers back from years of injury

going through the gestures long imagined.
And when you blew the candle out, it was

as one atop a birthday cake, lit only for the
silliness of blowing it back out again.

Miss Scarlet, questioned by Professor Plum, dissembles about suicide

Easier, of course, to
say that it was cancer
so the pity could be pure
instead of curious

Was it the husband
in the living room with
slippers on and
cotton in his ears

the child in the driveway
with the sprinkler
hooked up
to the garden hose

the doctor with the tiled floor
dispensing orange-colored caplets
in orange-colored vials
who committed nothing

at the wrong time
or committed not enough?

III. FALL

"For a moment it seems to be at a loss what to do,
till instinct begins to operate and directs it to its proper element ..."

Family recipes

Pearl had hoped that English
would be round and whole
inside your mouth.
She never made you learn Chinese.

You told me once
while I was chopping onions
that kittens, blindfolded for
too long a time when they are small,

will never learn to see.
She sang to you in lullabies
you couldn't understand.
Onion bringing water to my eyes.

I could not decipher it, your story
of the kittens with the eyes that never open.
As if you, too, kept a language
I had lost before I breathed.

On the outskirts of Knossos

Rented a room where the walls were white
and furnishings were spare
and Isidora the pensioner sat outside
in a plastic lawn chair, eating apricots
and sunflower seeds, exchanging news
with other ladies in chairs with seeds and fruit.

We spoke in eye contact and gesture
and in currency. Isidora left with the sun,
carrying her chair away, and I went up
upon the roof to string out my underwear
to dry, lace like fireworks of independence
across the blackened sky.

Silence echoed down the road where Isidora
was not sitting. I slept and when I woke
I could not move or see, though I felt a presence
in the room, the way one senses without
vision, without touch, that they have said something
irredeemably cruel and can never take it back.

In my terror I fell back asleep, and
when I woke again the room was still
and white and spare, and Isidora had yet to come.

I sat down by the roadside window,
waiting to catch sight of her carrying her chair
like a shell upon her soft and wrinkled

hermit body, praying that she would arrive
before I evaporated into imperceptible slickness
upon the white, white walls.

O O O

What are you? I asked the boy waiting in the brocade armchair in the hallway outside of class. He blinked slow, like he didn't have an answer at the ready.

I thought it was a data point just like your address or your parent's job, one of any number of things a kid had better memorize to answer strangers' questions and to fill out forms. Never occurred to me to mind.

And anyway I understood—the compulsion to reduce, reduce, reduce. To encircle the insect and then pin it down, your sharpest tip through its most central point, so its wings were frozen flat and wide and perfectly observable. It's what I was trained for.

Sure, I might have liked to be like something prime, refusing fragmentation of every kind. But I knew I was as even as an unpeeled orange, seams of pith along my careful halves.

Meet cute

We kissed on a Grecian Isle,
where you scooped a bloom of
bougainvillea from off the ground,
only slightly battered from the road,
and slid it in my hair behind my ear.

I crawled into your narrow hostel cot
and the older woman from the bed
across the room came over to explain
such things were against the rules.
I told you I was nineteen because

I thought it sounded elegant and old,
and you told me you'd saved long years
for your pre-thirty walkabout.
You were tired now, didn't want to keep
on moving, didn't want to go back home.

We said goodbye with your mouth
full of smoke. Every year you'd message
with a photo of a hammock on a beach
or a kitten on a balcony above an orange-
roofed city down below. *Come to visit,*

you would say. And I would send *haha*s
from my twin-sized bed, and a smiley face,
flattered you remembered me.
You wrote again, and wrote again,
asked me for a picture, or a sign of life.

I have a boyfriend, I wrote back,
no need to message anymore.
You wrote back right away. *Ok,*
no need to be a prudish cunt about it.

Last stand

Smoke unspooling in the sky
iridescent as an oil spill
as we drove down I-5.
Watched it lift before it spread

like a woman stretching in the morning.
Cry of a discordant recorder split
the silence in the car—*Take
your medications and your pets*

the cell phone notice says, *and
leave the rest behind.* From the highway
we cannot hear the water glasses shatter
on the hardwood floor or children

bump their shins upon the stairs.
Cannot see the aging dog lie back
down in his corner bed. Refuse to rise
at the calling of his name.

IV. BURROW

"They can descend as low as their instinct directs them, and certainly do ..."

Miss China

Aunt Jane said that in Asia,
I look like a child of war

Funny, I had thought myself
some kind of proof of peace

Fourteen at the airport in Shanghai when
the man with glasses took my picture

I thought—*I must be a looker here,*
but maybe he thought

I looked like the contrail
of a virile jet passed overhead

Cover letter

Crisis actors on the news again—
how do I become one?

Go ahead and slather me in ketchup
until my hair is shredded kelp along my temples

I can look into the camera making polygrams
of grief, or lie there in stunned silence

I remember nothing, there is no invisible thread
that ties each moment to the next

each one is brought forward alone
on the slaughterhouse floor

o o o

I'd grown up on *Where the Sidewalk Ends.* The
book lived on my shelf long after I'd outgrown
it and I never cracked it open anymore. I could
only see the spine, and sometimes, when rear-
ranging things, that cover—little kids curled
over themselves in black and white, the crum-
bling pathway stretched over a void.

It sat on my bookshelf next to journals where I
began writing about polar bears and about tak-
ing up less water, less electricity, less oxygen,
less money, less time, less money, money, mon-
ey.

My mind was like the untrained puppy that,
left alone, begins to shred things and to scratch
things, and defecate and cry. Best not to let it
get too bored. Best to tire it with runs in the
park, elaborate tricks, training to be best in
show.

Nothing I dreaded like the unscheduled day. I knew by the end of it the walls would be marred with claw marks, the carpet ripped up in the corners, the whole place rank with the odor of waste.

I had tried to explain it once to Jenny. We were trudging around ancient cities in the snow, cracking sidewalks slushy, roads of battered cobblestone. I tried to say that somehow I'd lost track—What was the point of everything again? I couldn't quite remember. I was sure somebody old and wise had told us once, but what in God's name had they said?

Everybody thinks those thoughts sometimes, she said, readjusting her scarf with her gloved hand. *But we can't think and talk about it all the time.*

Why not? I had wanted to ask. *Why would we ever do anything else?* But I could tell that she was tired and it was hard to talk about it without crying anyway.

A man came to an assembly once and spoke about being suicidal. *Nobody wants to die*, he'd said, *they just don't want to be alive anymore.*

And I had understood. I didn't want the side-
walk to end, I just didn't want to keep on walk-
ing.

Nineteen

I heard Pearl would throw the kitchen plates
and tease her hair up into beehives.

Sew gowns like ones in magazines
and speak like somebody born elsewhere.

That she was up too high and down too low
and it was February when they found her

on the ground. And when I felt the earth
begin to warp and I was slipping from the shore

I would scream aloud in empty rooms,
rail against the porcelain-crested waves

and beg the foreign, ancient gods:
Please do not mistake us.

Déjà vu

Mom hovered in the doorway
of the room that once was hers.

One thing that dead parents do
is leave the house to you.

What am I doing? I had asked her,
thinking maybe she would know.

How come I'm always failing?
My back against the wall

that now was mine, striped
in paints of every color.

My mother didn't often cry.
But sometimes when she laughed

hardest at the kitchen table,
her face would flash to red and

her features would slip out of their places
falling so far down that I

would think that she was sad.
You think you're failing? she said slowly.

How do you think   this makes me feel?
She stood there in the doorway

looking like I had just told
the sharpest joke she'd ever heard.

V. CLIMB

"[The] pupa found at the bottom appears to be well-formed, though all its parts are not entirely unfolded ..."

O Ô O

You'll come for tea, he calls from his shop as I walk by with a heavy bag. The next morning I pass by again. *Are you here now for your tea?* he asks. And again, when I return. *Now you will come*, he says.

I sit down at the table in the left corner of his shop and ask him questions. *Yes*, he tells me, *I've lived here in the Old City all my life. My father's shop, my grandfather's shop before him. Let me get the tea.*

The dresses on the walls are dripping from their hangers. The chess sets and Damascus boxes sit in disarray. He is a rounding, balding man. He comes back with two glass cups full of mint leaves in faded yellow water.

He pulls from his desk a thick round of bread and a dish of graying spices. *Take it*, he says. *Take it, take it.* The tea bags in the cups begin to dye the water amber. He is divorced. *Marriage*, he tells me, *is the great mistake.*

Where are you from? Ah, quite far away, yes, quite exotic. Have you siblings? Do they have boyfriends? He pulls out a hardboiled egg. *Take some, take some. Take some. Only if you want.* As he peels his egg I see he has six fingers on each hand.

I tell him my sister has a boyfriend and I do not. He returns to it. *What is your boyfriend like?*

Oh no, I say, *I don't have one. My sister does.* Later he returns to it again. *Your boyfriend, how do you know him?* The third time he asks, I tell him that we met at school and are in love.

As we talk, he calls out to passersby, invites them to please, come in and look. The black and white of my dress is garish here. Brown or burnt orange would be much better suited. *The tea, of course, is free*, he says.

If you want to leave something, leave it for the widow that I look after, that is all. Only if you want. Only if you want. I place all my coins upon his table as I leave.

The next time I pass by he does not see me or does not invite me in.

Open Closed Open

You gave me a book with an orange cover
and transcribed a line of it on the front page
in a navy felt-tipped pen

about being condemned to live
in the real world,
with no chance of parole

I thought it was the most romantic gift
I'd ever receive

I was awed by the caverns within you
how I could scream into your mouth
and hear it echo back out through your ears

waves refracted off of chambers
whose trap doors had all been sprung
I thought: *This must be love*

to hover at the edge of someone else's
darkness, trying by echolocation
to be sure exactly where you stood

Lacuna

I can hear the highway from
the bedroom on the second floor
the conch shell sound of heading home
and leaving home and passing through.
It's loudest when the cars are few
and light is gone or on its way
and *the highway is mine* for every driver.

I lay here all day waiting for the whisper to subside
moment like the flicker of a minnow
when nobody was on their way to any place
when the asphalt would lie flat along the sky
and I would only hear the thrumming of my blood
in the hollow of my ear.

2 a.m. on Gray's Inn Road

You had tonsillitis, and I was on the first day of my cycle
when I bleed the most and ache in every direction

You'd slept terribly for days and missed me at the train
because finally, blessedly, you got to bed

The dorm was small, bathroom like a bucket on a sailboat
but the picture window took up a whole wall

And when I woke up in the twin-sized bed
the sky was silver and the city covered in a fallen constellation

I perched up on my elbows, and as I came back down, you,
still in your sleep, raised and lowered your arm to make room

For my shifting body, and I knew then that I loved you
and I lay awake in silence, waiting for the chance to tell you so

Untitled

When my cousin visited
the condo in Ocean City
in the fall, the wind
rose up one day and
rattled all the storm
windows and porch grates
like so many chimpanzees
humiliated and afraid

She told me she rode
the outside elevator down,
turned left toward the ocean
and a stream of air,
compressed between one
building and the next,
lifted her clear off the ground
in its urgency to spread
its shoulders once again

She feared for a moment then
that she would die, but
listening, I told her no,

Delia, it's just like that,
the moment in the dream
when I know finally
I am on the verge
of understanding everything

VI. EMERGE II

"It first appears at the surface of the earth in the pupa or grub form, almost defenceless and very imperfect ..."

O O O

I was twenty-nine when the cicadas came back.
I was back in town for Pop-Pop's funeral, a
sparsely attended, solemn affair. Pop-Pop, my
godfather, had taken in my mother and her little
brother when both their parents died in quick
succession. He had been a colleague of her fa-
ther, Pei.

He had charged them room and board, which
my mother, who was only eighteen then, had
never quite forgiven. But she was very dutiful,
and she tried not to let him know.

Pop-Pop only had a story or two for my sis-
ters and me about the grandparents we never
met. Like one where Pei spoke in a stilted pid-
gin, or one where he followed a woman out of
Lord and Taylor, straight into the parking lot,
because she was so beautiful.

Anyway, when Pop-Pop died it was spring and
I was twenty-nine and the cicadas were out on
that hot Baltimore day in the graveyard.

They were mating in their hideous manner on the trunk of the tree above the sunken grave, and I saw one clinging to the shirt of the woman in front of me in a graveside fold-out chair. I covered my mouth and pointed it out to my boyfriend but he shushed me.

Later my boyfriend would help to shovel dirt over the casket until it was invisible, since nobody else was really young enough to do it, except for maybe me and my little sister, but no one thought to ask us. He had met my godfather once or twice.

I never really understood the whole cicada thing. Where did they go for seventeen years, and why bother to come back, and how did they know that it was time?

How could they possibly know that it was time?

Miss China II

Took a long time to admit I wasn't white
because my skin was fair and I never had
much trouble with the white boys

because Pei had bled out on the table
and Pearl had died by suicide
and we only saw Auntie like once a month or so

And my grandfather was white
and all the cousins gathered by the oceanside
and I had never met a person over twenty-five who looked like
    me

I had thought you had to feel something to be it
be held there in the chalky hands of somebody
whose hair was gray or gone

O Ô O

We stood on Mt. Nebo and I felt like I was
drunk or maybe glowing. We read of poor,
sweet Moses stammering up there for the
crowd.

I didn't grow up on much religion, though Aun-
tie was a Gideon who I pictured slipping crim-
son Bibles into cabinets in hotel rooms.

But I felt something holy there, in the valleys
and the peaks, the patchwork gray green gold
of it. I thought maybe I saw Magdala, home of
Mary Magdalene, from way up there.

I hadn't really understood that he, Moses,
would lay eyes on it but would never go, never
cross over the threshold for himself. Would just
see it from a distance in a haze.

Moses, who had raised his staff up over Egypt
and summoned a blanket of black locusts.
When white settlers came to my hometown,
they called cicadas locusts, certain they must
be a sign from God.

I don't actually believe in promised lands. Milk anywhere can curdle, bees everywhere can sting. But it was quite a story, and I was glad to be up there with you.

I wanted to grab both your hands in both my hands and keep turning around and around until we both grew dizzy from taking in every direction all at once.

I wanted us to see if it was true, that you could see the future without a swift and cryptic death. That you could look back without turning into a statue of salt.

Parallax

You told me I was your media-naranja,
that we were each halves of an orange

made round and whole together.
No, I said, resisting, *there must be a metaphor*

that makes us each whole on our own.
We cast about for something that let us be one

but also two, closed the distance
and also kept it there.

Maybe we are eyes, I said, *each one*
a sphere, alone, and when placed together

a new dimension becomes visible.

o ◊ ○

I lost the black bound journal from the year I climbed out of the ground. I lose lots of things, I guess, but it's the only journal that has ever disappeared.

Sometimes I think I remember what I must have written there—something about how I thought I had to crack every code, and realized finally no, it was me who had to crack. Or did I read that somewhere?

There was therapy. There was medication. There was boxing. My mom, who forced me to make a doctor's appointment, then came with me to give the family history. Nana, my father's mother, who said, *Don't worry, I'll read all those books with you so you don't have to read them all alone.*

But somehow all the breadcrumbs that I dropped myself are gone—like I was followed by a naughty dog who snapped them up, strange scattered treats.

Like the Minotaur found my clever ball of yarn, unraveled it to so much fuzz while she made her quiet way behind me.

VII. MOLT

"The process by which they extricate themselves from the slough is slow at first, though soon finished ..."

○ ○ ○

When my older sister Jenny turned thirty and then had a baby, it was time to bleach my hair and try some psychedelics. You and I ordered them by mail and they came in handsome packages with brightly colored stickers over top.

We ate them on the beach one day, and you began to retch while I lay still and wondered if I needed to take more because nothing much was happening. But soon the colors and the shapes of things began to swirl.

And my hat was made of sand, my face and features twisted like a nightwalker painted by Picasso. You wanted to speak, to share the things that you were thinking and were coming now to know. But I wanted just to lie there as the ocean and the sky spiraled together and the insides of my eyelids became panels of stained glass.

Later we walked down the beach to the snack shack and bought a lemonade, giggling to keep the teens behind the counter there from knowing we had misplaced all our edges. We walked back holding hands and a seagull, walking slow in front of us with his deliberate orange feet, didn't balk as we came right up close behind him.

He knows, I said to you, and you agreed. *He knows we can be trusted.*

Confession

Killed the National Figure
camped in my amygdala
begging to be born

Rolled her flat as marzipan
then thinner still, till she lost
all her flavor and her grip

Had to scrape the rest like
shit from off a flip-flop
against the pebbly cement of
what is here

Where the sidewalk ends

The seminary students passed me on the road
sermon due at 12:15

The only man who stopped for me seemed
like he carried pockets full of free time

Wouldn't he be late? I asked him as he took
a bag from out of my arms and I put back on my shoe

Nothing less holy than a rush, he said

I blushed, and he blushed to see me red
handed me my bag and walked off at a measured pace

I dropped my bag again, let apples roll out
on the road and lay prostrate for a time

Begging forgiveness of the asphalt and the soil

O Ô O

The year the cicadas returned, I left Brooklyn and a job. We made a spreadsheet with pictures and prices for everything that had to go. We kept the comforter cover, the books, the rice cooker I had gotten as a birthday present.

Gave away the desk and chair, assembled end tables into fleeting stoop stores. Bagged up all our half-used spices, posted them online until a neighbor came, who said they would be perfect for teaching her teenagers how to cook and then took them all away. She looked Chinese to me.

I cried in a Zoom farewell party, and we got in the car. It was a car I had crashed twice before to make it partly mine.

My family was always moving east. From Shanghai through San Francisco or Chicago, finally to Washington, D.C. From Texas to St. Louis and then onward to New York. If you tilted a globe on its side and carved a little trench along the mid-Atlantic coast, that's where all of us would eddy.

We tilted back the globe, dribbled our way through Pittsburgh, Lafayette, Kansas City, Spanish Peaks, Santa Fe. My hair had all its pigment still stripped out, except for up along my skull, where it was growing back in black. When I arrived at the other ocean, I dyed it back an imitation of my abandoned color.

I told my therapist I wasn't doing much these days. *It's kind of like you're finally going through your adolescence*, she said.

I blinked my eyes to say I'm sorry, come again?

When you look at all the things that you received and shake them for yourself, to see if they hold true—you know, like rebellion.

Aren't I a little old for that? I asked. She shrugged.

I called my mom. *What do you think?*

My mother laughed. *Yeah, it's like you're thirty going on thirteen.*

Something about the way she said it, I knew it was a compliment.

Mary Wayte Community Pool

East of here, a little pool
lanes roped off with plastic
red and black. The women
gather naked in the shower

tell each other of the broken
furnace, the husband who can't
leave his chair. Dead mother's estate
to be divvied up and sold.

They stink of chlorine. They
have dimples on their asses
and the backsides of their arms.
That's not good, they say.

I know it, say the others.
They pull back on their
socks and sweaters, wear their hair
out dripping in the cold.

Back into their SUVs on
intricate suburban roads,
itching for the next time
the way forward will be straight

and the prize for going on
is arriving back at the beginning.

VIII. GENERATE

"They survive only two or three days after they have performed their respective parts in the process of generation ..."

O Ο O

The waiting room was darker than outside—so much so that the street beyond the glass-paned doors was blurred out by the brightness streaming in. I hadn't been to see a doctor in a few years. The receptionist on the left side of the waiting room was occupied.

A small, old woman sat facing me in a chair to my right. An old man in a blue shirt sat next to her, a cane resting just inside the armrest of his chair. The little woman looked up at me where I was standing near the entrance.

Thank you for your patience, she said, gesturing toward the woman at the front desk talking with the staff. *She is my interpreter.*

No problem, I said and shifted my weight from my right leg to my left. I was not in any rush today.

I must have glanced over again—noticing the polka-dotted silken scarf tied carefully about her neck, the tidy white bandage around her right hand, her hair white and gray up at her roots, the rest of it died imitation black.

She looked like she might have been one of the women who did tai chi in Sunset Park, or a woman like Auntie who tied up laden glass casserole dishes within red, patterned handkerchiefs to keep them warm. Looked like the kind of woman who might, like my mom, think it rude to return a borrowed dish without more food inside it.

She looked up at me again and caught my eye. *Thank you*, she said. *For your patience.*

Of course, I said, louder this time. *No problem at all.* I tried to smile widely to show her how unperturbed I was, how perfectly content to just keep standing there, swiveling my femurs in their sockets. But my mouth was hidden behind a paper mask.

She stood up from her chair. I undid my sideways slouch. Standing, she came up to my breastbone. She moved closer to me and I bent forward a degree.

I fell today, she said, and held forward her bandaged hand. *I am old. I am eighty-six.*

She spoke slowly so the numbers could send ripples out, heavy stones dropped into quiet ponds.

Not good, she said.

I'm so sorry, I said, nodding forward just a little more. *That's not good.* I meant the fall and not the growing old, but I forgot to specify. She shook her head and looked away.

Her blue-shirted husband rose from his seat, leveraging his cane against the floor to stand. The interpreter had finished at the desk and had come back toward the couple. It was my turn to sign in now.

You are a nice lady, the old woman said. *A pretty lady.* And with a nod she took small steps past me toward the door.

I twisted back to watch her exit. *Good luck,* I called, and she turned to nod again, and maybe smile, but her mouth, too, was covered up in paper.

The glass-paned door swung slowly shut, tracing wobbly shadows in the outdoor light cast on the ground. I wished I had tried to say something in Chinese. *She must have known from my eyes*, I thought. Surely my eyes had given everything away.

I wanted to call out to her, *Pópo, my family—they call me Mei-Mei!*, but she had long since vanished in the light.

Likeness

When Nana died at the dining room table
I knew that she was gone because her bottom eyelids fell away.
Underneath the iris there is white.

They told me on the West Coast that the moment the sun has
Tugged the tail of its skirt down with it, there's a flash of green
Among the sherbet colors.

In the watercolor class, the teacher paints the shadow on the
    paper sphere
To help roll it off the page. He leaves a crescent moon of
    brightness
At the bottom of the globe, says it's the reflection back of

Every other thing within the room.

Topanga

The girls who live downstairs are
parceling enlightenment on Instagram

and I am naming every flower on my daily walk—
black sage, cobweb thistle, mustard.

We're just the same, all on the cusp of our Saturn returns,
each assembling our almanacs of proof.

Daisy chains we'll wear like flotation devices
when the tide comes rolling in.

O Ô O

My boyfriend, who grew up on the West Coast, said he'd never seen cicadas before that hot day in the graveyard. It had never occurred to me that they didn't show up everywhere in their inscrutable, prime-numbered cycles. I decided it was time to look them up.

I read that after those long years underground, tunneling in the mud and living off of xylem, they quickly have to shed their skin so they can learn to fly. For a few hours, after they discard the skeleton of childhood, they are very easy prey. Their body hasn't hardened yet, so they are, for a while, tender helpless things whose wings are not yet ready.

When they do get off the ground, their flying is clumsy. They are always running into things, clanging their chubby hammer heads against the brick and concrete world.

They come out above the ground to mate of course. To search for one another so that they can hatch their tiny nymphs. And before long the fragile babes will fall out of the trees and roll back into the dirt. But nobody is quite sure how they know that it is time. Must be something in their genes. They think it might be the same thing that tells the birds the time is coming to head south, that tells the salmon the time has come to swim back up the locks.

The same thing that tells people it is time to leave home and then return, to cast away the stones and then to gather them. To unravel every last forbidden stitch and then to knit it all back up again.

Before dawn

Dog woke us up at four a.m. again
crying by the door, pleading to be let into the dark.

Outside, frantic, he catches shoots inside his mouth,
but leaves every flower standing, whole,

just runs his tongue across the sleeping lawn.
Once when I was sleeping on the bottom bunk

I staged a teary resistance against sleep—
Why won't you go to bed? my father asked.

Because I don't want to get older, I had said,
and I don't want to die.

IX. HATCH II

"We found only a solitary instance of the last melancholy note of an expiring race, to be found no more for seventeen years ..."

Pearl,

I want to ask you—why that day? Once I heard a writer say that the day of the story must be different from all other days. Something like Passover.

What were you afraid of? Did you leave a note? I never asked anyone. I never thought to ask. I don't think it would have been appropriate.

And did you ever think of me? Imagine me? Have ideas about who I was supposed to be? Did you want me to be a doctor, too?

I would like you to know that I have been afraid of you. That I don't know too much about the soft and tender moments.

I do know you ordered Coke in glass bottles to be delivered by the kitchen door underneath the breeze-way. Breezeway is gone now, just so you know.

Did you know whenever I am home I use the bath-room that was your bathroom? But the house looks different now. Not a lot, but a little.

Once I tried to sketch it from memory and I left out a whole section of it—forgot the part where the kitchen is.

I read a book the other day that said Chinese people communicate about their feelings in their food. I actually don't know if you were much of a cook.

I assume you were. That you made pork shoulder. That you took my mom to the Chinese grocery stores in Rockville, the ones that smell of stewing cabbage.

Near where I'm living now there's this place called Uwajimaya. Actually it's Japanese, but it's where people seem to go. I bought eggroll wrappers there for Chinese New Year.

It doesn't smell like a Chinese grocery store. It smells like Whole Foods. Inside it looks like Whole Foods, too.

There's a Whole Foods now on River Road, near the MotoPhoto. I don't know what was there that you'd remember. Did MotoPhoto exist yet?

Our member number at the swimming pool is still 50 though—isn't that a hoot? Hard to imagine you in a swimsuit.

I've only seen a few pictures so it's hard for me to imagine you in anything really. I can't do the 3D rendering in my mind. I would need to have seen you from more angles.

I want you to know that Mom is doing well. I think you would be proud of her. She is really something. She's so solid. Doesn't crack.

She became a doctor, like you always wanted. But I sort of think what she wants more than anything is to be a good mom. And she is, Pearl. She's a great mom.

Sometimes I remember how you spooked her, though.

Once in an Intro to Evolutionary Biology class, they pulled up this graph of sonic niches in a jungle to demonstrate how we evolve and specialize our songs to be heard.

So if the cicadas take the high notes with their pulsing and their clamor, the bullfrog will go in a long and low hum; each can take up soundwave space without colliding.

And anyway, sometimes I think you made Mom feel like she couldn't be up high, like she couldn't go down low, because those were your terrain. You took all the highest notes, and you took all the lowest ones, so everyone else was left to carve a home in the thrum and droning of the middle.

I'm posted up in bed today. I heard you'd do this sometimes, when an emotional affliction overcame you.

I've heard that you were jealous. That you thought Pei's desire to be famous was vanity and a chasing after wind. Which is funny because the man your daughter married, and their three daughters, too, are chasing just such windy things.

I've heard the story of how he, Pei, followed you out of Lord and Taylor because you were so beautiful. I thought that story was romantic.

Now I sort of wonder if you were flattered or afraid as you heard his footsteps in the parking lot behind you.

You had been abandoned once. Maybe that's why you were jealous. I heard your parents left you behind when they came here for the first time. You were small and a little like an orphan in Shanghai. Though I guess that you had Auntie.

And later they came back to get you, but they had to fudge your birthday on the paperwork since they'd lied upon last entry about your existence and false-hoods, like every living thing, insist upon their own survival.

Most. Most living things.

I wonder if every time you wrote down your American birthday, it was a reminder of those long years left behind.

The way I understand it, after you died, your parents kind of receded from view. I guess they wanted nothing to do with you anymore.

My dad said they met Jenny once when she was born, maybe when her eyes were still a murky blue, before they hardened into brown. But they never met me, and never Lizzy.

Had you forgiven them before you died? I don't know if they'd forgiven you before they did.

For what it's worth, Pearl—Should I call you grand-ma? Wàipó?—I forgive you.

I don't really know about the others. I don't know about Mom. I assume so, so much time has passed, but I don't know for sure. I guess that I could ask. Would you like me to ask?

I can imagine how death must have clung to you, close as the white of an egg to the yolk. How you burrowed after death as if maybe it would let you breathe. How you felt—but in a way that didn't feel like feeling, masqueraded as a knowing and a certainty—that you could not keep walking.

Mom didn't talk too much about you growing up. Fragments scattered here and there. But I know she still misses you. Remembers your American birthday. Remembers you the day you died.

Growing up, she cooked us dinner every night. Knew all the recipes in Auntie's cookbooks: lion's head, five-flavored shrimp, cooked fish with their heads still on and eyes wide open. Once she said she learned to cook when she was young, maybe twelve or so, because you were stuck in bed, not well enough to rise for dinner.

Maybe I've remembered wrong. Maybe she did talk about you. Maybe she was talking about you all the time in a language I am only learning now to understand.

A bit funny doing this now, Pearl—befriending you—when for many years I wanted to be as far from you as possible. I suppose what I wanted was for us not to be related.

Maybe I'm just older now, and not so scared.

Sometimes I wish you'd had a chance to be old, to grow rounded in the back, and wrinkled. To hold both my little hands inside of yours.

But I think it's sweet and strange that I was there inside the womb growing inside of yours. That you're stitched up in my mitochondria, quiet as an insect waiting long years in the unsuspecting mud.

Pearl, imagined II

You should remember this,
she said. *You might never*
see it again.

Sitting on the patio, February
buds like grains of rice
along the branches.

She is always saying
things like that. As if tomorrow
the apple will collapse

into the little hollow
at its core, the oxygen will
condensate back into lye.

I pick at a cuticle to
keep my eyes from rolling. She smiles.
I just don't want you

to be caught off-guard.
We watch a squirrel skirt the yard.
He knows, she says, as we

watch him take flight, cling to a trunk
like it's the one soft thing
in a world made of wire.

Acknowledgements

Thank you, Lisa Pegram, for being the godmother of this book, ushering it into being and then editing it into maturity. I am grateful for the unrelenting love and rigor you have gifted me and my work since I was seventeen years old. Both my writing and I are better for it.

Thank you Carmen Peters and all other members of the Jaded Ibis Press team for making this project a reality.

Pieces of this work were written in two formative workshops: Jennifer S. Cheng's, hosted at Kundiman, and Annie Liu Kellor's at Hugo House.

Emefa Agawu, Rose Nguyen, and Addie Tsai: your close reading and incisive feedback (and also your encouragement) helped this work become itself.

Thank you to dear friends who cheered me on and talked things through with me, in particular my oldest writing companion, Camylle Fleming; the "wolf pack;" Maggie Horikawa, Ellie Shechet, Mili Cima, Emefa (again); and new friends in LA who met in coffee shops, went on walks, and helped me navigate forward.

Thank you to my many poetry teachers, from elementary school through college.

Glenn and Lisa, without your generosity and support I would never have had space to write this. I am grateful to be able to call you and the extended Blumstein/Zaidi clans my family.

I am grateful to the extended Holland, Shen, and Pao families. Nick and Allison, thank you for pulling the Shen family together again to learn about the past, and to all those who've shared at our reunions. I am grateful to those family members who are no longer with us but show up in my memory, in my imagination, and in these pages.

Jenny and Lizzy, thanks for being my best friends and early readers. How lucky the three of us got to share a childhood. Mom and Dad, thank you, for everything. You've made it all possible. Thank you especially, Mom, for going on this journey with me. I am very grateful to be your daughter.

Finally, thank you, Ben, for always holding out the hope that I would make things, for your attentive reading and wise suggestions at every stage, for being the other eye that gives the world its depth and shape. I love you.

Printed in the USA
CPSIA information can be obtained
at www.ICGtesting.com
JSHW050242230324
59561JS00013B/46

9 781938 841255